HS

6

101 Facts About

EXOTIC
PETS

Published by Ringpress Books Limited,
PO Box 8, Lydney, Gloucestershire,
GL15 4YN, United Kingdom.

Design: Sara Howell

First Published 2001
© 2001 RINGPRESS BOOKS LIMITED

ISBN 1 86054 231 X

Printed in Hong Kong through Printworks Int. Ltd

0 9 8 7 6 5 4 3 2 1

101 Facts About

EXOTIC PETS

639.3

Julia Barnes

Ringpress Books

1 Do you have a taste for the exotic? Well, you don't have to travel thousands of miles to see some really fascinating creatures. Many will live very happily in a home called a terrarium.

2 A terrarium is a glass tank with a tightly-fitting lid. Small gaps in the glass called **ventilation grills** allow fresh air to enter.

3 The type of home you create within the terrarium will depend on the needs of the creature you are keeping.

4 Slimy or scaly, dull or brightly coloured, slow-moving, slithering, or quick as lightning, there is a huge number of different pets you can keep in a terrarium.

5 Reptiles and amphibians are the most popular terrarium pets. For those who like the creepy crawlies, tarantula spiders are a good choice.

6 **Reptiles**, which include turtles, lizards and snakes, and **amphibians**, which include frogs, toads, **newts** and **salamanders**, come from two different families, but they are sometimes jointly known as **herpetofauna** or **'herps'**.

7 All herps are cold-blooded (they cannot keep their own bodies warm). But apart from that, reptiles and amphibians have very different lifestyles.

8 Reptiles (like the iguana, pictured above) have a thick, scaly skin which protects them from cuts and scratches.

9 Most reptiles produce their young from eggs. The offspring emerge as miniatures of the adult, and can immediately look after themselves.

10 The name 'amphibian' comes from the Greek words meaning 'two lives'. This is because amphibians (like the newt, pictured below) live both on land and in water.

11 A female amphibian will lay jelly-like eggs in the water. The offspring start life in the water, and they move on to land when they can breathe air.

12 Amphibians have very delicate skins, and they must live in damp conditions.

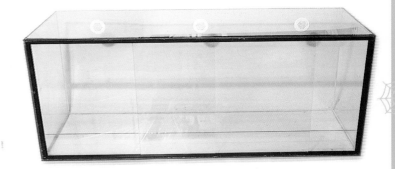

13 If you are keeping a reptile or an amphibian, you must create the conditions that are as close as possible to those in the wild.

14 The terrarium (pictured above) gives you the opportunity to make a mini world, providing the correct temperature, and suitable land or water features for your pet.

15 Making a few basic changes within the terrarium, you can create a desert, a tropical forest, or a **semi-aquatic** set-up which is half land and half water.

16 The first, and probably the most important job is to get the temperature right for the creature you are keeping.

19 A **thermostat** should be used to control the temperature in the terrarium to make sure it does not get too hot or too cold.

17 Warmth can be provided by a heat mat (pictured above). This is placed under the tank, and should extend over one-third or one-half of the terrarrium floor area.

20 The sun sends out **ultraviolet rays** which are vital for the health of many lizards and turtles. A specially-made fluorescent light tube, (pictured below) will provide this type of light in your terrarium.

18 A spotlight (pictured right) can be used for basking – the reptile's version of sunbathing.

22 The bottom of the desert terrarium should be covered with sand or gravel. This surface is known as the **substrate**.

23 Use your imagination to create a desert-type landscape with rocks. You may be able to get some desert plants but make sure these do not have any spikes.

21 Some lizards, such as Leopard Geckos (pictured above) and Bearded Dragons, like the hot, dry conditions of a **desert**. The temperature under the spotlight should be 97 degrees Fahrenheit (31.5 degrees Centigrade), but it should fall to 68 F (20 C) at night.

24 A small saucer of water should be placed in the desert or 'dry' terrarium.

25 The **tropical forest** terrarium provides a complete contrast to the desert. It will suit some of the more exotic tree frogs (pictured right), lizards, snakes and tarantulas.

26 A tropical terrarium hot-spot should be around 90 degrees Fahrenheit (32 Centigrade), dropping to 75 F (24 C) at night. A cooler area should also be available.

27 A tropical climate is hot, but it must also be damp.

28 A surface of bark chippings, a layer of moss, plus a bowl of water will keep the conditions moist. You will also need to spray the terrarium with a light mist of water at regular intervals.

29 Many of the tropical snakes, lizards and frogs spend their time in trees, so you will need to provide some branches that reach to the top of the terrarium.

30 A semi-aquatic home (pictured below) will be needed by most turtles, newts, a

number of frogs, and some snakes. The temperature will depend on the type of pet you are keeping, so seek advice.

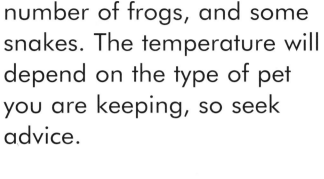

31 You will need a special underwater heater. Turtles like a temperature of 75-81 degrees Fahrenheit (24-27 Centigrade), but amphibians prefer it cooler.

32 The terrarium must be split into a land area and a water area. You can use rocks at one end, and create a slope to the water.

33 It is a good idea to cover the rocks with moss so the more delicate amphibians and turtles do not injure themselves.

34 A fluorescent light tube should be fixed into the roof of the terrarium, and positioned so that it is above the land area.

35 A number of snakes, such as Corn Snakes (pictured right) and Milk Snakes, do not like conditions to be as hot or as dry as a desert, but they do not like the hot, damp conditions of the tropical terrarium. Their home, often called a **savannah** terrarium, can be changed to suit their own special needs.

36 The temperature in a savannah terrarium should range from 75-86 degrees Fahrenheit (24-30 Centigrade), and it should be sprayed a couple of times a week to keep conditions reasonably damp.

37 A savannah terrarium needs more cover than in the desert set-up. Rocks and cork bark (pictured below) are ideal for this. Plants tend to get eaten, so plastic plants (pictured right) are a good choice. The best substrate is a coarse gravel.

38 Before you rush out and buy an exotic terrarium pet, you must make sure you know as much as possible about the creature you are going to buy.

39 Most importantly, you must find out how big it will grow. The danger is that you will buy a small youngster, and before you know it, your pet has outgrown its home and is too big to handle.

lizards, and they can both make great pets. However, a Leopard Gecko measures around 10 ins (25 cms), and a large iguana can be as big as 7 ft (2.13 m) so needs lots of specialist care.

40 A Corn Snake, which measures 3-4 ft (0.91-1.22 metres) is an excellent choice; a female Burmese Python which grows up to 20 ft (6 metres) could become a major problem.

41 A Leopard Gecko and a Green Iguana (pictured above) are both

42 Terrarium pets have different needs when it comes to feeding, and you may find some more difficult to cope with than others.

43 Plant-eaters or **herbivores** include iguanas, and some members of the skink family. They eat green food and fruit.

44 Most of the lizards (like the Bearded Dragon, pictured below right), and nearly all the frogs and toads eat insects, and so are known as **insectivores**. The most common insect food is crickets. These are usually available in pet stores that sell reptiles.

45 Fruit flies are the best food for small frogs and some salamanders. Earthworms and slugs are enjoyed by most of the salamanders and newts.

46 Snakes are **carnivores** which means they eat meat. Pet snakes are fed mice, rats and chicks, which they usually swallow in one gulp.

47 Most baby snakes are fed on a diet of day-old mice or rats, which are known as '**pinkies**'.

48 There are around 3,000 species of lizard, but you can cut that number right down when it comes to choosing a terrarium pet.

49 Green Anoles (pictured below) are the most popular of all the lizards. They come from southern USA, and are sometimes known as American chameleons.

50 They are not related to chameleons, but they can change colour. A green colour shows they are contented, but if they feel threatened, they become dark brown.

51 Green Anoles like a tropical forest terrarium, and, as they live in trees in the wild, they need tall branches to climb. They live on a diet of insects.

52 The average size of a Green Anole is 9 ins (23 cms), and they prefer to live in small groups.

nocturnal – sleeping during the day and becoming active at night.

53 The Leopard Gecko (pictured above) is an ideal pet for beginners. They are easy to look after, and should live for at least 15 years.

54 These boldy-patterned lizards come from India and Pakistan. They are insect-eaters, and do well in a desert terrarium. They are

55 Most members of the gecko family have sticky toe-pads, but the Leopard Gecko (pictured below) has a cat-like claw at the tip of each toe.

56 The Bearded Dragon (pictured below) is a lizard that comes from the hot, dry areas of Australia, and it is another choice for the desert terrarium.

57 The name 'bearded' refers to the large spines around the chin and throat, and along the sides of the body. When the Bearded Dragon is in danger, they fan out, making him look fierce.

58 Bearded Dragons grow to around 20 ins (50 cms), and although they mostly eat insects, they also enjoy leafy green vegetables and fruit, which should be offered every other day.

59 The skinks are one of the largest families in the lizard group, with over 600 different species. A total of 17 different skinks are found in North America.

60 Most skinks grow to about 12 ins (30 cms). Some are bigger, like the Blue-tongued Skink (pictured above), which measures around 20 ins (50 cms). This skink is named after its blue tongue which it will show when it hisses.

61 A tropical terrarium will suit most skinks. They like a deep substrate of bark chips or soil covered with moss, and their favourite food is earthworms.

62 Spiders are not everyone's first choice, but they have their fans. The Pink-toed Tarantula and the Chilean Rose Tarantula, who are both insect-eaters, will do well in a tropical terrarium.

63 The Pink-toed Tarantula (pictured above) is black with pink areas going up from its toes. It is a great climber and will build a web in the branches of a tree, which it will use like a hammock.

64 The Chilean Rose Tarantula (pictured right) likes to burrow, and so it will need a deep substrate of soil and moss. Hiding places should be made from wood bark.

65 There are 200 different species of turtles which belong to a group known as **Chelonians**. A shell covers most of the body, and the turtle will withdraw into this at times of danger.

66 There are four different types of Painted Turtle which all live in the USA. Each is brightly coloured, with splashes of red and yellow on an olive-green background.

67 A semi-aquatic set-up will be needed for Painted Turtles, who like to spend time in shallow water, and then climb out on to the rocks.

68 Although they eat snails and worms when young, Painted Turtles eat more plant food as they get older. Most Painted Turtles will live for up to 15 years.

69 The Box Turtle (pictured below) comes from the eastern USA. In the wild, it spends most of its time on land, so it is happy with a savannah set-up plus a dish of water.

70 The Box Turtle's shell can close up completely when it is in danger. It can stay closed for several hours before the turtle needs to stretch out its head to breathe.

71 Box turtles have an incredibly long life span – they have been known to live for up to 125 years.

72 You either love them or hate them – snakes are certainly the most exotic of all the exotic pets.

73 The Corn Snake (pictured above) is the best choice for beginners.

74 Corn Snakes adapt well to terrarium life. They like warmth and they will use a bowl for bathing.

75 Garter Snakes (pictured right) generally live near water. They are small and beautifully patterned.

76 A Garter Snake needs warmth and easy access to water. They also need fish, which can be provided by feeding a complete diet.

77 The Milk Snake (pictured above) grows to around 3-4 ft (0.91-1.22 metres). They are often found near cattle sheds.

78 It was thought that they drank milk from cows, but, in fact, they stay near cattle because rats and mice live close by.

79 Snakes do not need feeding every day. For example, an adult Corn Snake or Milk Snake will need to be fed every 14 days.

80 Frogs (pictured above) and toads are members of the **Anura** family of amphibians, which means they have no tails.

81 Frogs and toads share the same amazing cycle of reproducing themselves. After eggs have been laid in water, tiny tadpoles hatch out.

82 Like fish, tadpoles (pictured below) breathe through gills. To begin with, they live entirely in water.

83 The process of a tadpole becoming a frog or a toad is known as **metamorphosis**. At first, the gills disappear and the lungs take over. Then the front limbs start to develop.

84 Young tadpoles will feed on tiny green plants called **algae**, but, as they get bigger, they will need to eat small worms.

85 It may take several weeks or several years for the change from tadpole to adult to be completed.

86 The Green Tree Frog (pictured right), is one of the most popular types of frog to keep. They are light green in colour, but become darker if the temperature drops.

87 As they live in trees in the wild, you will need to provide lots of tall branches and plants for them to climb.

88 In the breeding season, males have a loud call which sounds like a duck. They often call just before a storm, and have become known as 'rain frogs'.

89 Salamanders and newts are amphibians with tails, and they belong to the **Caudata** family. There are differences between them, but scientists refer to them both simply as salamanders.

90 The main difference is that newts (pictured above right) spend a large amount of their adult life in water, whereas salamanders leave the water once they are fully grown and then live on the land. They return to the water to breed.

91 Salamanders (pictured far right) are often mistaken for lizards, but, unlike lizards, they have a smooth, moist skin and no claws. They can live in much cooler temperatures than reptiles.

92 Most salamanders are more active at night. But in salamander terms, that does not mean a lot of rushing about. During its lifetime in the wild, a salamander may not move more than a mile.

93 Salamanders can shed their tail if they are attacked. The lost tail soon grows back. In fact, the salamander can lose a toe, or even a whole limb, and grow it back.

94 There are many different species of salamander. Fire Salamanders (pictured left) and Tiger Salamanders (pictured above) both adapt well to terrarium life.

95 Fire Salamanders need a land set-up with lots of hiding places. A bowl of water must be included.

96 In contrast to their name, Tiger Salamanders are not fierce. They are less shy than most Salamanders and can become quite tame.

97 Red-spotted Newts are found throughout the eastern half of the USA in the wild, and they are sold in pet stores as 'green newts' or 'common newts'.

98 The European Common Newt (pictured below) lives in damp, moist areas on land, coming back to the water to breed. The female may lay as many as 300 eggs.

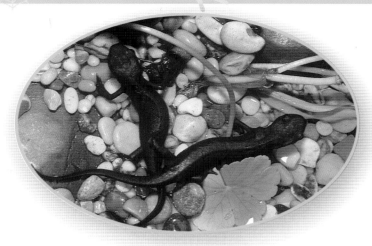

101 You may think that you have now found out a lot about exotic pets – but this is just the beginning. There is a wealth of fascinating facts about each of the many exotics – and the more you know, the better you can look after your terrarium pet.

99 Fire-bellied Newts (pictured above) get their name from the fiery red colouring on the underside of their bodies.

100 They like a semi-aquactic environment, with an area of dry rocks so they can leave the water when they wish.

GLOSSARY

Algae: tiny green plants which form on the sides of a tank.

Amphibians: a group which includes frogs, toads, newts and salamanders.

Anura: frog and toad family.

Carnivore: meat-eater.

Caudata: the family which includes salamanders and newts.

Chelonian: the turtle family.

Desert: a hot, dry region.

Herbivore: plant-eater.

Herpetofauna ('herps'): a name for both reptiles and amphibians.

Insectivore: insect-eater.

Metamorphosis: the process of a tadpole becoming a frog or a toad.

Newt: an amphibian that spends most of its adult life in water.

Nocturnal: a creature that sleeps during the day and is active at night.

Pinkies: day-old mice or rats.

Reptiles: a group which includes turtles, lizards and snakes.

Salamander: an amphibian which spends most of its adult life on land.

Savannah: a hot, dry region, but with more plants than a desert.

Semi-aquatic: half land, half water.

Substrate: terrarium surface material.

Thermostat: a temperature control.

Tropical forest: a hot, humid region that has lush plant life.

Ultraviolet rays: a type of light that comes from the sun.

Ventilation grills: small 'fresh air' gaps in the terrarium.

MORE BOOKS TO READ

An Owner's Guide to a Happy, Healthy Pet: Leopard Gecko
Lyle Puento
(Hungry Minds Inc.)

All About Your Snake
Chris Newman
(Ringpress Books)

Look and Learn: A Basic Book of Amphibians
W. P. Mara
(TFH Publications)

Your Bearded Dragon's Life
Liz Palika
(Prima Publishing)

WEBSITES

About spiders
http://insects.about.com/science/cs/
spiders/index.htm

Geckos online
www.3rdimension.com/Leopard/

Newt and salamander care
www.netwave.ca/~large/
newtsal.htm

Bearded dragon heaven
www.lizardheaven.com/bearded.htm

To find additional websites, use a reliable search engine to find one or more of the following key words: **terrarium pets**, **tarantulas**, **bearded dragons**, **snakes**, **turtles**, **geckos**, **salamanders**, **newts**.

INDEX